THE
## Irresistible
## Church SERIES

# Are You READY?

## A **PERSONAL GUIDE** to **DISABILITY MINISTRY** for the **RELUCTANT LEADER**

by Mike Dobes

 THE IRRESISTIBLE CHURCH SERIES

*Are You Ready?*
Print Edition ISBN 978-1-946237-08-8
Kindle Edition ISBN 978-1-946237-09-5
ePUB Edition ISBN 978-1-946237-10-1

Author: Mike Dobes
Contributing Authors - Ryan Wolfe and Gina Spivey
Collaborator -  Bret Welshymer
Contributing Editor - Ali Howard
Editor in Chief - Eric Jones

Printed in the United States of America.

Produced by The Denzel Agency (www.denzel.org)
Cover and Interior Design: Rob Williams

For information or to order additional print copies of this
and other resources contact:

Joni and Friends International Disability Center
P.O. Box 3333, Agoura Hills, California 91376-3333
Email: churchrelations@joniandfriends.org
Phone: 818-707-5664

Kindle version available at www.irresistiblechurch.org

# CONTENTS

*On the contrary, the parts of the body that seem to be weaker are indispensable, and on those parts of the body that we think less honorable we bestow the greater honor, and our unpresentable parts are treated with greater modesty, which our more presentable parts do not require. But God has so composed the body, giving greater honor to the part that lacked it, that there may be no division in the body, but that the members may have the same care for one another.*

1 CORINTHIANS 12:22-25

# To Fully Belong

Deep within the human soul is the desire to be wanted, to be valued, to matter. There is a profound cry within each of us to fully belong. What does it feel like to fully belong? What does it truly mean? Imagine with me, for a moment, life within an authentic community where the walls of our guarded hearts can come down, where honesty and acceptance reign, and where each person is valued for his or her unique gifts and abilities. Does this seem more fantasy than reality? According to author Robert M. Hensel, "there is no greater disability in society than the inability to see a person as more." I invite you to dream with me as you read this book—to discover the heart of God anew and his plans for the Church to become the pure spotless bride as promised in the book of Revelation. Can you picture a place where people gather in the name of Christ without discrimination—a place where the abilities of individuals are celebrated without comparison. All people are welcome, all people are embraced, all people fully belong.

All too often, our churches have closed doors, raised curbs, stairs, and other obstacles that keep people affected by disability from attending and participating. Unfortunately, it is not uncommon for a single mother of a child with autism to feel confined to a solitary playground on Sunday mornings instead of attending church where she wants to be. Where does the former pastor who has become a quadriplegic through a tragic accident attend church when both physical and social ramps do not exist? Consider the young girl with spina bifida who desperately wants to believe that God loves her and has a purpose for her life, yet she is unable to find a church that welcomes her with open arms. What if, when we prayerfully consider how to make our churches more "attractive" to the community, we realized that there are many people who desire to attend if only we would remove some obstacles?

This is the heart of an *Irresistible Church*—to be a place where people are celebrated simply because they are created in the image of God and have an indispensable place in the body of Christ. This type of church is defined as "an authentic community built on the hope of Christ that compels people affected by disability to fully belong." An *Irresistible Church* finds a way to remove obstacles and minimize hindrances, resulting in a wonderful mosaic of people with all abilities worshipping and serving God together. The boy with autism encourages others through his impressive gift of memorization; the girl with Down syndrome makes every person feel cared for as she greets them at the door. The man who uses a wheelchair teaches youth group and shares his testimony of discovering God in the midst of great suffering. The young lady born blind leads worship using the beautiful voice with which God has gifted her. Is this not the church that Christ envisioned when he gave his life as a sacrifice? Is this not a church that would exemplify the love of Christ to a world sorely in need of a Savior? Is this not a church that provides the hope and encouragement we all need to make it through the day? Let us together build *this* church so that all may come in and know Christ.

**Perhaps you are a pastor who received this book from a parent or volunteer at your church.** This is not a condemnation or critique—it is a heartfelt plea to open the doors of your church a little bit wider so that people of all abilities might participate in fellowship and worship together. I invite you into the wonderful journey of disability ministry. It will be filled with challenges and heartaches; victories and setbacks; sorrows and joys. You might be thinking, *That's a description of ministry in general.* You are right! Disability ministry is just another beautiful expression of God's love for his people. This type of ministry can be intimidating and foreign if you aren't familiar with it—I know because I too am a pastor who simply didn't get it until I was introduced to the vision and mission of Joni and Friends. Now, I see the need. And gratefully, God has transformed my heart to consider people affected by disability in all I do. Disability ministry will completely change your heart; it will positively influence your walk with Christ, your sermon prep and, ultimately, the congregation you are called to lead. I invite you to embrace the world of fully belonging.

**Perhaps you are a ministry leader or volunteer who is unsure about disability ministry.** Becoming an *Irresistible Church* is more than a program or activity. It is about the heart of the leaders and the attitude of the church. It is about making space for *people of all abilities* to be fully included and celebrated in the life of the church. The Bible clearly speaks to this issue and commands us to care for those who have been marginalized. Thank you for your heart to lead and serve in this ministry—you are making a difference simply by reading this book. Please allow the words on these pages to challenge and inspire you to serve families affected by disability well.

**Perhaps you are a family member affected by disability.** Allow me to encourage you that there is hope like never before within the church. God is starting a movement of churches across the world that are opening their hearts and doors to people affected by disability. I pray that his grace would overwhelm you today, and that reading this small book would provide a glimpse of the hope you have been searching for. Pray for your pastors, your leaders, and your church. Pray that the heart of God for your family washes over your church, and that God moves you from a place of marginalization to celebration.

Together, we can see the church embrace people of all abilties as God intends. This book provides a biblical foundation for disability ministry, speaks about how individuals affected by disability fit into the Body of Christ, and addresses the heart of pastors and ministry leaders. Are you ready to be stretched? Are you ready to assess your own heart and consider what God might be calling you to?

Let us explore this calling and see the church become an agent of change as we reach the entire community with the gospel. The truth is, we are all affected by disability. Whether personally, through a family member, or a friend...or maybe simply the understanding that sin is the ultimate disability. I am walking this journey alongside you—an enthusiastic pastor humbled by how God has opened my eyes and softened my heart. Thank you for joining the movement to become an authentic community built on the hope of Christ that compels people affected by disability to fully belong. Thank you for endeavoring to become an *Irresistible Church*.

# A Biblical Foundation
# for Disability Ministry

Before considering any aspect of ministry, we must consider the heart of God. If our endeavors are not ultimately grounded in the Word of God, they will be based upon our strength and simply will not last. However, God's Word accomplishes what he desires, and it will not return void (Isaiah 55:11). The Bible is our source of hope, encouragement, and strength. It reveals the heart of God and salvation through Christ. In the pages of Scripture, we hear his voice, and learn of God's plans for our lives. It is here our journey to fully belonging must begin. Let's take a look at a few passages of Scripture to lay a firm foundation.

Luke 14:21b, 23 – *"Go out quickly to the streets and lanes of the city, and bring in the poor and crippled and blind and lame . . . and compel people to come in, that my house may be filled."*

There is much that we can learn from this parable. One purpose of Jesus sharing this story was to reveal God's desire for those who have been marginalized to be fully embraced and welcomed at the banquet table. Christ is using strong language to communicate how the church should function. It is interesting to note that this exhortation includes the urgency to be done quickly. Christ tells us that we must intentionally reach out to those who have been marginalized and cast aside by society for his house to be filled. The church looks most like the bride of Christ when it is reaching, serving, and embracing the lost. Many of our friends affected by disabilities certainly fall into this category— whether they have never heard of or received the gospel message, or they are followers of Christ looking for a place to fully belong. The leaders of the church must become the culture-benders that do not merely tolerate people affected by disability, but rather welcome them into an authentic community where they may fully belong.

1 Corinthians 12:22 –*"On the contrary, the parts of the body that seem to be weaker are indispensable."*

How often do we let our own brokenness and humanity affect how we view and value others? I can relate to Samuel who was called to anoint David as the next king of Israel, but was tempted to anoint David's big brother based upon his size and charisma. God constantly reminds me that it is more about heart and character than appearance. As we welcome the entire body of Christ into our assembly, the blessings gained are immeasurable. In this passage, Paul challenges our perspective of others, reminding us that everyone is created in the image of Christ. Therefore, their abilities carry far more weight than their disabilities. I deeply desire that as the body of Christ we would see people as God does, looking for ways to embrace and serve one other, rather than considering only what others might accomplish for us.

Blessings from God often arrive in unexpected packages. A young man who is non-verbal might take longer to communicate a story, but it teaches us the valuable lesson of slowing down to "listen." A little girl with Down syndrome may love to hug and embrace everybody around her without prejudice, bringing a special joy to her church that is otherwise missing.

I was profoundly blessed when shortly after meeting my new friend, Alex, he asked if he could pray for me. Alex has cerebral palsy and, at times, it is difficult for him to make his thoughts known. As Alex prayed, I leaned in to discern the nuances of his speech. My personality typically keeps me from standing in one place for too long, but I was captivated by the heart of this young man. His prayer stopped me in my tracks, focused me on Christ and left me in tears. I was humbled by his heart for God, and I learned in that moment the rich blessings I could gain through my friendship with Alex.

Ephesians 4:15-16 – ". . . *we are to grow up in every way into him who is the head, into Christ, from whom the whole body, joined and held together by every joint with which it is equipped, when each part is working properly, makes the body grow so that it builds itself up in love.*"

Again, we see that the heart of God is for the *whole body* to be joined, held together, and built up in love. This is simply not possible if members of the body are excluded, whether through intentionality or lack of awareness. It would be a tragic misunderstanding if the phrase "working properly" somehow became an excuse to only include people who seem healthy or whole. According to David Guzik, "This means every part and joint provides what it can supply in a coordinated effort." He also notes that "God wants us to see the church as a body, where every part does its share."[1] People affected by disability have purpose from God, provide value to his body, and are important, contributing members of the church. We often do not realize that our churches are incomplete and that parts of the body are missing. However, as we allow everybody to fully belong, we cannot help but be blessed and encouraged as others are able to worship God and serve him in various ways. The church cannot truly function as it should until it understands the value of embracing those who have been shunned and marginalized by society.

2 Samuel 9:13 – *"So Mephibosheth lived in Jerusalem, for he ate always at the king's table. Now he was lame in both his feet."*

This is the ending of a powerful Bible story. You might be thinking, *Who was Mephibosheth?* Allow me to give you the highlights of his story:

- He was the son of Jonathan, grandson of King Saul, and the heir to the throne of Israel according to his royal lineage
- He had become disabled due to an injury as a child
- He was homeless and in hiding because he feared that David, the new king, would have him killed
- He was a societal outcast due to his physical disability and the relational tensions

So, how does Mephibosheth's story relate to our calling of becoming irresistible? David modeled what it means to be an authentic community built on the hope of Christ where people affected by disability fully belong. When David learned about Mephibosheth, he found out where he was living and sent for him (Luke 14). He spoke value, purpose, and love over Mephibosheth's life (Ephesians 4:15-16), and he fulfilled a promise made to his best friend, Jonathan. Mephibosheth was not tolerated or humored by David; he was celebrated, he was embraced, he was allowed to fully belong. May each of our churches be filled by the "Mephibosheths" of our community. May they be allowed to dine at the table of the king and share the value they possess (1 Corinthians 12:22).

1 Corinthians 12:12, 14 – *"For just as the body is one and has many members, and all the members of the body, though many, are one body, so it is with Christ. For the body does not consist of one member but of many."*

Disability ministry is about coming alongside people affected by disability to serve, encourage, and celebrate their personhood. When we consider our physical bodies, it is amazing to see how God designed us to adjust when parts are missing or injured. There are countless stories of people overcoming the odds to find success in varying fields despite, and sometimes because of, their disabilities. Do our churches provide the same opportunities to excel for individuals affected by disability? Do we work to fully embrace all people and welcome them into the body of Christ? We are doing a disservice to people affected by disability, to our churches, and to God when we exclude and marginalize parts of the body. The heart of the church is incomplete when it is unwilling to embrace and celebrate individuals affected by disability. Their absence might be a result of inaccessible facilities or a lack of programs, but more often it is a heart issue within our churches. We naturally gravitate towards those who think, talk, and act like we do, sometimes shunning those who are different. But when we do this, we fail to experience the beauty of learning from our differences. Consider the impact of serving on a missions trip in a foreign country. Often, the experience is heightened due to the cultural differences between nations. In the midst of serving people that we think are so different from ourselves, we learn that our similarities outnumber our differences. When we spend time with and listen to others, their unique perspectives, experiences, and feelings bring us great insight and expand our appreciation of life.

So, what can people affected by disability offer to our churches? I believe they offer the same things that people not affected by disability might offer—a heart of worship, an understanding of God, and a commitment to pursuing Christ. Everybody has skills and talents, passions and gifts that contribute to the overall well-being of the church body. Having a physical or cognitive disability should, in no way, diminish this fact. The gifts of the Spirit are not limited to those who "fit in" with our programs and ministries. They are not limited to those who might navigate a church platform without assistance. They are not limited to individuals without sensory issues. Rather, *"as each has received a gift, use it to serve one another, as good stewards of God's varied grace."* (1 Peter 4:10, emphasis mine)

In addition, 2 Corinthians 9:8 *(NLT)* reminds us that *"God will generously provide all you need. Then you will always have everything you need and plenty left over to share with others."* The body of Christ is complete when members are not only able to receive the gifts that God has for them, but to generously share those gifts with others inside and outside of the church environment. Too many of our churches are missing out on the abundant blessings that are wrapped within the lives of people affected by disability. We often see brokenness suffering, and disability first – this skews our ability to see the image of God in every man, woman, and child.

Jesus died on the cross for salvation – not just for the Jews, but for all people.  It is through his sacrifice that all are welcome, all are included, all are celebrated. It is worth repeating that everybody has purpose, everybody has dreams, and those who might seem weaker are truly indispensable members of the church. We are compelled by the God to make space for them; not merely a seat on Sunday mornings, but by opening the doors to ministry, servanthood, and leadership. The body of Christ reflects God's will when all people are evangelized and discipled by the Word and disability is not a hindrance. Let us come together, make every reasonable accommodation, and see our churches become the community that God originally intended.

**Note**

1. https://www.blueletterbible.org/Comm/guzik_david/StudyGuide_Eph/Eph_4.cfm?a=1101016

# The Body of Christ

The most basic definition of leadership is influence. Whether you are a senior pastor, a ministry leader, a volunteer, or a parent (or any combination of these), your leadership is about the people you influence and how they respond. Influence is powerful, and you have the capacity to make a difference for generations to come. Influence can be good or bad. In order to share God's grace with those we serve, we must embrace his grace in our own lives. His grace paves the way for all people to be included, for all people to be welcomed, for all people to have a place of belonging in our churches. My prayer for myself, and for everyone reading this book, is that the grace of God will guide our leadership and our influence on others.

So, what are some of the ways that God might use disability ministry to influence your church, your families and your community?

- **Your Church**—We have already established that the church is not really complete unless we are including and embracing people of all abilities. The gospel is intended for every tongue, tribe and nation. Until our churches compel people affected by disability to fully belong, there will be a gap. The mission and health of the church is dependent upon everybody being able to not only experience God, but also to use their gifts to encourage and inspire others.

What if your church became known as a place that welcomes people affected by disability? Perhaps your friends affected by disability could serve as greeters and ushers, perhaps they could teach a class or lead a small group. It is not uncommon for individuals affected by disability to worship God with inspiring passion—could they remind the rest of your church what it looks like to worship for an audience of One? Regardless of what it might look like, the heart and character of your church will change for the better as all the members of the body fully belong.

I spent many years leading and directing church camps for both children and teenagers. These years were filled with powerful moments of worship, discipleship, fun, and life transformation. I look back on that season with great fondness and appreciation for all that God did in the lives of thousands of kids and, by extension, their families. I now have the privilege of leading one of Joni and Friends' *Family Retreats. Family Retreat* is one of the ministry programs at Joni and Friends where families affected by disability are able to come to receive respite, refreshment, and rest. We provide activities, worship, Bible teaching, and time to connect to others. It is a week where families are encouraged to not apologize for anything because they are embraced right where they are, and they are able to fully belong. After all my years of camp experience I can tell you this: what God does at *Family Retreats* affects me in a personal way far beyond anything I experienced in my years of children's and youth ministry. I have learned, and continue to learn, that suffering causes emotions to become more acute. Whether joy or pain, frustration or peace, when we have experienced deep suffering, our emotional experiences are forever changed. This causes highs to be even higher and lows to be even lower, but it also allows for a bonding and friendship that go beyond the typical.

Each year, I come to *Family Retreat* with the intention to serve and bless families, but without fail I walk away feeling like they blessed and encouraged me far more than I did them. When I witness uninhibited worship expressed through song and dance with no regard for what others might think, I am reminded that God cares more about my heart than my appearance. When I have a friend affected by disability pray for me, it brings tears to my eyes because it reminds me that our relationship with God is not inhibited by our brokenness. I spend far too much energy attempting to hide my brokenness while my friends simply approach God knowing that he genuinely loves them as they are. When I see pure joy radiate from parents as they witness their children experience love and acceptance, there is nothing this side of heaven that compares. I am privileged to experience this slice of heaven for one week at a time during camp, but imagine what your church could look like if life is done together every week.

- **Your Church Family**—Families affected by disability spend countless hours and energy navigating the education system, the medical system, the therapy system, and the list goes on. What would it look like if they could attend your church and not feel like there was a list of items to navigate? What if church was not another place where they felt like a burden, but instead was a place where they were loved, cared for and even celebrated?

  Many families affected by disability that I have the privilege of doing life with are tired and worn out. They are weary of the pressure our society places on them, and exhausted from the energy it takes to navigate life with a disability. A simple task for me, like attending church, is often a big endeavor for families affected by disability. If they are not part of an *Irresistible Church* where they can fully belong, the effort to attend might outweigh the return on investment. I am constantly in communication with families who are desperate for a church community that will love them, work towards accessibility, and include them in all facets of church life. Does this take some work on the part of the church? Absolutely, but how can we refuse to put forth the effort when we are talking about valuable people created in the image of God?

Simply by engaging in disability ministry, you speak value to the familes you serve. Your church becomes a place of hope, love, and peace. It becomes a place where the presence of God is experienced through tangible acts of service. Families will feel safe. They will have a community to turn to for prayer and support, as well as celebration and joy! And if your church is able to serve and welcome one individual or one family, the ripple effect will spill over to other family members and friends as they share their experience of being welcomed by the family of Christ. The eternal and lasting impact of this decision cannot be measured, but I know that it will influence generations of people for the kingdom of God. It leaves me in amazement to think of the potential impact of serving just one family!

• **Your Community**—There was a time when our churches were the physical center of every community. Towns would build the church first and expand from there. What would it look like if your church was once again in the center of your community? Would you be a place where people felt more grace than criticism? What if your church was known more as being for people than being against issues? Disability ministry has the potential to create such an impact that your community would truly miss your church if you were gone.

Our world needs the hope of Christ. All of the therapy, programs, networks, and other support tools for families affected by disability pale in comparison to the gospel message and the opportunity to experience relationship with the God of heaven and earth. We become hypocritical when we preach a message for all people while closing the door to those who don't "fit" our expectations. As God's heart for the disability community permeates your church family, it can't help but spill out to your community. Families would know where to go for prayer, for acceptance, for a place to fully belong. Your church would become a powerful advocate for the many people who have been marginalized by disability. You would become the beacon of hope that so many families are desperately searching for.

Let's see what some practical expressions of this community influence might look like.

## A Heart for Community

The point of the gospel is offering salvation to the lost; those who are not right with God have the opportunity to be reconciled through Christ. Salvation is bigger than ability or disability; it is a sin issue. In the same way, our churches should determine how they can be welcoming to the entire community, affected by disability or not. What does it look like when a church truly cares about their community? There is a frequently repeated quote in the church world: If your church closed or moved, would the city notice? How much influence or impact does your church have on your city, or does it connect only with those who are already Christ followers?

If the heart of the gospel is to "seek and save those who are lost," then your church should be looking for ways to make a difference in the community at large. It cannot be a club for believers, but ought to be a place where Christ followers are trained and equipped to engage others with the message of salvation and reconciliation. People affected by disability are often an overlooked group that desperately needs the hope God provides. Will your church rise up to go out into the community and invite people affected by disability to dine at the table? Are you willing to lay aside your personal comfort or expectations for your church in order to serve others who are without Christ?

A heart for the community looks for ways to come alongside people who are marginalized, providing support, encouragement, and resources. An *Irresistible Church* desires authentic relationship with the local community with the goal of sharing the hope of salvation. A heart for the community takes on the posture of Christ who laid aside his rights in order to perfectly serve a broken world through the cross. This is what God calls us to as members of his church. Disability ministry is simply a pathway to serve others, to open the doors of your church a bit wider, to compel people affected by disability to fully belong. A heart for the community does not ask, "Lord, should we?" A heart for the community declares, "Yes, Lord. Here we are, send us!"

Below is a list of potential community influence opportunities for your church to consider as God continues to transform your heart:

*Sensory Movie Outreach* – Partner with other local churches to rent out a movie theater in your area and hold a "sensory-friendly" movie event. Many theaters will be glad for the opportunity to better serve families affected by disability and may only charge the actual rental fee for the film. At this type of event lights are generally left on, attendees are free to get up, move around, and interact with the movie. Churches can provide bags of goodies and snacks or other support resources for attending families.

*Christmas Gift Giving* – If your church provides a gift-giving event for families in need, try to include games, toys, and other Christmas items that are disability friendly.📖 You may even consider opening the event early for families affected by disability—the opportunity to "shop" with smaller crowds and greater accessibility will be a valuable blessing to them.

*Respite Events* – A monthly night out for parents and caregivers can be a huge blessing to families and

📖 This symbol indicates that there are supplemental resources that correspond with this topic at http://irresistiblechurch.org/library/

might provide an open door for them to eventually attend church. In the *Irresistible Church* book *We've Got This!* you will find details and practical training tips for churches to begin and expand respite events. Consider inviting youth and college groups to serve as buddies during the event. Other groups in your church might be willing to provide a dinner or other practical helps for parents. Ideally, local churches will network with one another, providing respite events on different days or weeks so that families affected by disability have multiple opportunities for respite.

*Church Holiday Events* – When hosting special seasonal events, many churches open their doors early to the disability community. These kinds of events could include Harvest Festivals, School's Out Parties, Easter Egg Hunts, or Christmas Celebrations. An extra hour or two designated exclusively for families affected by disability allows the crowds to be less overwhelming, increasing their chance of enjoying the experience. An additional idea for Easter would be to provide "audio Easter eggs" for children with visual impairments. These eggs chirp or beep, allowing everybody to participate in and experience the hunt.

*Video Welcome* – You can work with your church staff or volunteers to create videos of what to expect at church. This kind of video might include a tour of the church building, introductions of key people, and clips from various classes or worship services. These videos can be posted on your website for all to see. Social stories are a wonderful tool to accompany these videos and can help to ease anxiety for those planning to attend for the first time.

*Practical Helps* – Many families affected by disability could use help with chores, home maintenance, or even driving assistance. Similar to providing meals for families with a newborn baby or a family member in the hospital, providing practical help is a tangible expression of Christ's love. Church members can come alongside families affected by disability to wash their cars, perform household chores, and provide car maintenance.

*Use of Facilities* – If your church has a large building or multipurpose facilities, consider how sports fields, gymnasiums, and rooms could be used for the benefit of the disability community. Could your church provide rent-free options to day programs, thereby building a wonderful bridge between your church and your local community? Sporting events, awards ceremonies, parent support groups, and independent service providers could benefit greatly from this type of partnership, thus providing even greater support and community for families. Not only does this serve the greater community, it also provides a simple way for families to come onto church property that may otherwise never visit.

*Community Collaboration* – You can partner with local disability service groups in the areas of art, theater, job training, and placement. With these organizations you can host dance recitals, theater productions, and employment programs. You might even look for existing providers who are interested in opening a day program or employment program at your church facilities during the week.

*Special Olympics* – Recruit and send members of your church to serve as coaches for your local Special Olympics leagues or other similar organizations within your community. Consider hosting a BBQ or other gathering to celebrate athletes before or after a competition.

*Dances and Proms* – Check with your local YMCA, Boys & Girls club, or other civic organizations to see if they are willing to partner with your church to host a special dance or social night. Connecting with local high schools and colleges for volunteers can be a great idea.

# The Heart of a Leader

As God calls and equips leaders, he is looking for those who reflect his heart and communicate it well to those he or she leads. Perhaps you feel like Gideon who was probably glancing over his shoulder, frantically searching for somebody else when the angel declared, *"The Lord is with you, O mighty man of valor"* (Judges 6:12). Gideon was unable to see how he could possibly make a difference in the face of such opposition, but it was more about what God saw in Gideon than what Gideon saw in himself. Perhaps you feel like David who was anointed at a young age but had to wait for what must have felt like eternity to fulfill the promise of becoming king. May I encourage you not to allow hindrances, struggles, or time pull you away from the heart of God for people affected by disability. Perhaps you relate best to the apostle Paul who was busy with his own agenda when God intersected his life in a powerful and transformative way. I personally relate to Paul. I was a pastor who had no understanding of disability. When God called me to serve at a week-long family camp my heart was touched and transformed by a young boy named Danny. Danny had Down syndrome, and I was his "buddy" for the week. When it was time to say goodbye, I realized that I would never be the same and that God was clearly up to something in my life. Has disability affected your family or friends to the point where you feel you must do something about it? Honestly, it doesn't matter where you are as a leader or how you best identify with disability ministry. I pray that ultimately your cry echoes Isaiah when he submitted to God by simply stating, "Here I am! Send me."

## Learn the Needs

I was single and in my twenties when I enthusiastically began serving in full-time ministry. I was a children's pastor who knew everything. Sadly, it took me quite some time, and courage on the part of a few parents, to help me realize that I was not truly meeting the needs of the families I was called to serve. Despite all my passion and energy, I had missed the mark. Why? Because I had never bothered to ask the families what their needs were. I turned my assumptions into facts and built my ministry paradigm on this faulty foundation.

Thankfully, by the grace of God, I slowed down and began to listen. I formed a parent advisory team for the children's ministry, and we began to prayerfully reshape the direction and style of the ministry.

Many years later, I was blessed to attend the wedding of a young lady who I pastored through her elementary school years. As I watched her and her beloved exchange their vows, I was humbled to see the fruit that can come when we are willing to set aside our own agenda and do things God's way.

As leaders, we must take time to hear from those we are called to serve. Whether or not you are personally affected by disability, it is far too easy to assume that we know what is best. This is partly because of pride, and partly becuase it is simpler and quicker to build something based upon assumptions. It takes time and energy to gather input from others and make changes based on their suggestions, but the process is worth it. Ask questions, listen, and ask God for wisdom to read between the lines when necessary. This doesn't mean that every thought and opinion from every individual should be acted on, but it does mean that we must listen and make every reasonable accommodation as we serve others.

In your effort to learn the needs of the families in your church, remember that each family will have unique needs. Be careful to work against any tendencies to lump people into groups based upon disabilities or other factors. Ministry will be more effective and sustainable with a personal focus, rather than relying on labels. As trust is built and families feel safe, they will connect more personally to your church and begin to invite their friends into the same experience. I believe when we go slowly and make ministry more about people than programs, we will be amazed by how God works in and through our churches.

## God's Heart

2 Peter 3:9 declares "the Lord is not slow to fulfill his promise as some count slowness, but is patient toward you, not wishing that any should perish, but that all should reach repentance." The heart of God is that all would come to know him and his saving grace. This is not limited to those without disability, but is a free invitation to people of all abilities. In light of this, we must recognize the heart of God and live accordingly.

First, God is most concerned about our relationship with his Son, Jesus Christ. He is not worried about our finances, our work or, any other component of life except within the context of how it relates to his Son. If God is this concerned about the souls of all people, should we not strive to have a similar focus? Our churches should always be about the gospel before anything else. Disability ministry without an evangelistic heart becomes well-intentioned childcare, youth program, or adult small group, but lacks an imperative eternal perspective. See John 3:16, Romans 5:8, and 1Timothy 2:4 for more biblical insight on this topic.

Second, God calls each of us to a life of righteousness, not because of our good works, but as an outflow of the grace that God pours into our lives (1 Peter 1:16, Deuteronomy 6:17-18, Matthew 5:6, 1 Timothy 6:11). Do you believe that this calling applies to everybody? Can an individual profoundly affected by disability still live a life of righteousness? Absolutely! Many of my friends affected by disability have a much better understanding of living in God's grace than I may ever have. Perhaps disability compels them to lean on God more. Maybe disability helps them realize what is truly important. I am not sure of the exact reasons, but I have much to learn from my friends in this area. I am not ashamed to implore you—will you please join me in working to ensure that our churches provide teaching and discipleship for *all people*?

Finally, God has a specific purpose for each of our lives (Philippians 2:12-13, Romans 8:28, Jeremiah 1:3, Jeremiah 29:11). Ultimately, this purpose is to glorify God, thereby advancing the kingdom of God in the lives of those around us. Purpose is not about skills, talent, ability, or anything else that I might possess. Purpose is about the God-ordained reason for each individual life. Our purpose is not to gather money, go to school, or even to have a family. While God may include these things in our lives, our purpose is to bring glory to God by doing what only we are able to do. As Jesus said, "In the same way, let your light shine before others, so that they may see your good works and give glory to your Father who is in heaven" (Matthew 5:16).

Unfortunately, we often confuse "purpose" with "skill" or "talent." We can make the assumption that good works must be accomplished or achieved to fulfill our purpose. This is a dilution of how our purpose might give glory to God. Consider the story of the man born blind in John 9. While religious leaders argued about who to blame for his condition, Jesus provided a profound response in terms of our good works. Jesus shared that the man's purpose, including his blindness, was for the works of God to be displayed in his life, creating an opportunity for people to see and believe. As I studied this passage, I experienced a profound shift in my understanding when I realized that the man's disability was the means by which God's glory was displayed. From this story, I think we can conclude that a person's physical or cognitive disability can be seen as a good work that will bring glory to God! This is a complete reversal of how we typically view suffering and disability. I must be completely honest though: I am not at a place where I can embrace this view of disability yet. Not even close! But I am drawn to this story and compelled to see my friends affected by disability as Jesus does. Truthfully, we are all affected by disability in some manner, and we have all been created to give God glory. The struggle in combining these two facts arises when disabilities are more overt and visible, prompting a level of awkwardness and tempting me to forget that all people are created in the image of God. This concept of God's glory in our weakness completely changes my understanding of purpose and has the potential to radically shift how I view, pray for, and interact with those who cross my path.

# **Allowing vs. Embracing**

I have held various positions in pastoral ministry since 1997: children's and youth ministry, young adults ministry, and teaching pastor. Over the years, there were many times when a family affected by disability attended our church. Gratefully, God gave me the eyes to see that individuals affected by disability were not a hindrance to ministry, and I tried to make whatever reasonable accommodations I could to include them. For example, one young boy, Corey, was nonverbal and a wheelchair user. The first day I met him and his mother, she asked with great hesitation if I was the children's pastor and if there was a place for her son. I enthusiastically replied yes to both questions, and we ensured that Corey had a spot in the front row so that he was able to see when the other kids stood up for worship, games, and other activities. Corey was part of our ministry for years, and to this day his family is still an active part of the church.

While this seems to be a very positive story, it personifies the idea of "allowing" people affected by disability to attend church. I never considered ways that Corey could serve. I never reached out to his family beyond Sunday mornings. I never worked to provide a platform where everyone in the children's ministry could see Corey's abilities before we saw his disabilities. While I would have never considered asking a family to leave church because of their disabilities, I also never considered the great value that they could contribute to the body of Christ.

Stick with me while I explain this concept of "allowing vs. embracing." Allowing might mean that while your church has programs for individuals affected by disability, their meeting space is in a back room, out of the way. Embracing on the other hand, might mean that your church leadership intentionally looks for ways that people affected by disability can interact with everybody and influence others. Allowing can become focused upon the details of a program while embracing is all about relationship and doing life together. Allowing is often dependent upon the schedule and convenience of those who serve. Embracing is about sacrificial love and preferring others before ourselves.

When I applied for my current role at Joni and Friends, I realized that I had never even heard of or considered disability ministry before. Over fifteen years of full-time ministry and I had not once thought about how many families were unable to attend church because of disability related obstacles.

Over the course of my time working at Joni and Friends, my perspective has changed. This shift happened primarily as I served during and eventually began leading a Joni and Friends *Family Retreat*—a week of respite and summer camp for families affected by disability. Through these experiences God has graciously moved my heart from "allowing" to "embracing." Embracing means that everybody has a place at the table, everybody has a gift to share, everybody has a purpose to fulfill. It is much more about relationships than programs. In the church world, we often confuse activity with ministry, and at the end of the day we are just busy. The call for an *Irresistible Church* is to assess our hearts, to do all that we can to welcome all families regardless of their abilities or limitations . . . and if we are able, to have a formal program that serves specific needs related to disability.

May I challenge you to not be content to simply "allow" people affected by disability in your church? Your life, your church's life, and the lives of people affected by disability will all be richer when "embracing" is the norm. We are all better together, and it starts with the heart, attitude, and atmosphere of our churches.

# Are You Ready to Fully Belong?

As you may recall, an *Irresistible Church* is defined as "an authentic community built on the hope of Christ that compels people affected by disability to fully belong." I am friends with a married couple who, to me, embody the definition of being *Irresistible*. They radiate the heart of God in such a joyful and contagious manner that I can't help but laugh and smile when I am around them. They pray for me, they love me, and they make me feel like family when I am in their home. Would it surprise you to learn that both of them are deaf? What if you knew that they have two sons with severe autism and a daughter who was recently diagnosed with ADHD?

Most people in our culture would likely look at this family with pity and sympathy, expecting that they have many needs and nothing to offer. And while they do have many needs, they also have much to share with those around them. They are filled with the grace of God and compassionately seek ways to love and be generous towards others. They live out the definition of *Irresistible* every day, and I believe they know and experience God in a far more personal way than I do. I often wish I could be more like my friends and less like myself! I will not tell you that the transformation to become *Irresistible* is simple or even desirable many days. Far too often, I am content in my self-focused life doing things as I have always done. Yet I know that God has called me into more. He has called me into authenticity, and vulnerability, and to live a life reflective of all that his Son has done for me. Regardless of the role you have in ministry, he has the same call for you. Don't be afraid to ask yourself hard questions, let the Spirit guide you as your heart undergoes surgery, and enjoy the blessings of becoming irresistible on a very personal level.

Several years ago, I was preparing to preach the welcoming message as the director of *Family Retreat*. I was interrupted during worship by a leader who hurriedly shared with me that one of our campers was in the off-limits lake. I didn't fully understand what she meant, so I looked over the porch of the sanctuary to lake. Seeing the still, calm water I began to fear the worst. Quickly, I removed my shoes, sunglasses, cell phone, and lapel microphone as the worship leader was instructed to "just keep playing songs . . . the speaker isn't ready yet!" I splashed into the water, still scanning the surface with no success of spotting our swimmer. Finally, his head broke the surface of the water about fifty yards out, clearly having the time of his life. I swam out to him as quickly as I could (wishing I was in better shape), and after what felt like an eternity, my new friend and I landed back on the beach.

Knowing that he was safe, and that our worship leader was probably out of songs, I ran to my room and changed quickly. I was trying to pull my thoughts back, trusting that God would remind me of what I had prepared to share. As I approached the sanctuary, I ran into the mother of my new friend. She was about to drive away from camp. Tears streamed down her face as she attempted to share how she was convinced that this was simply one more instance where her family was a greater bother than a blessing. I assured her that everything was fine, and that we loved her family. A distressed look came over her face as she realized the director was the one who had pulled her son out of the lake. She apologized over and over until I finally interrupted her, "You are no longer allowed to say, 'I'm sorry.' This is a week without apologies. We are family, and family loves and serves without hesitation." It became our motto for that week of camp that no family would have to apologize for any perceived inconvenience on their part. God never fails to take our stories of brokenness and transform them into tales of redemption, healing, and hope. That week became a wonderful memory for my new friend and his family, and years later God is still very clearly at the center of their lives.

To fully belong means that we are loved, embraced, and celebrated—regardless of our circumstances. It means that our disabilities and weaknesses are not criticized, or even seen as something to be fixed, but rather embraced as a part of who we are. While often seen as cliché, it is so very true that God's strength is made perfect in our weakness. The church is not intended to be a place where we revel in and boast about our perceived strength. Rather, it is a place where the broken, humble, lost, and marginalized may come together in a wonderful assembly that embraces people as they are, reflecting the gracious love that God has given to each of us. Where we lack, let us trust that God will fill the gap, both by his Spirit and by our church family. Where we are strong, let us trust that God will provide us opportunities to serve others. To fully belong means that we can be transparent with our struggles and our hurts without worrying that others will criticize or ask us to leave. It means that our churches become sanctuaries where we see ability before disability, grace before rebuke, and love above all. It is this heart and attitude that will transform our churches into places that overflow with the grace of God and move our churches back into the center of the community. Doesn't that sound irresistible?

God is on the move, and we see flashes of *Irresistible* transformation across the globe. Disability ministry will change the landscape of your church because it is not about a program, it is not about a staff position, and it is not about providing services. It is about being the body of Christ and truly loving people. There are no pretenses, qualifications, expectations, or standards in an *Irresistible Church* to receive the love and grace of God. The doors are wide open, and we simply say, "Come!"

My prayer is that you are beginning to see the necessity and beauty of embracing disability ministry. According to 1 Corinthians 12, the body of Christ is comprised of many people with unique gifts. The body would not function properly if we were all the same or each had the same giftings. This is not a matter of value or importance. I am not better because I am not affected by disability, neither are my friends better than me because they are affected by disability. Christ compels each of us to consider others first and to prefer others above ourselves. I believe that our churches are majorly missing out unless our doors are open so wide that all people, regardless of abilities or disabilities, truly feel welcome.

Are you ready to join me on this wonderful journey? Will you allow God to pierce your heart, make you *Irresistible*, and then help you to influence others to join in as well? The journey will be filled with tears and laughter, heartache and celebration, confusion and victory. But what life and ministry doesn't include these elements? At the end of the day, Christ died on the cross so that people from every walk of life would be included in his family, including those affected by disability. Throughout Scripture, God commands us to pay special care to people who have been marginalized by society (James 1:27, Galatians 2:10, Luke 14:12-14), and to build our churches as authentic communities that compel all people, including those affected by disability, to fully belong. I dream of a day when formal disability ministry is no longer needed because we are simply the church, fully embracing and valuing all people, regardless of abilities or disabilities.

# Becoming *Irresistible*

Luke 14 commands Christ followers to "Go quickly . . . find the blind, the lame, and the crippled . . . and compel them to come in!" While this sounds inspiring and daunting, exciting and overwhelming, motivating and frightening, all at the same time, what does it actually mean? How do we live and function within the church in such a way that families affected by disability are compelled to walk through our doors to experience the body of Christ?

We can certainly *compel* them by offering programs, ministries, events, and other church activities, but what if the compelling aspect was more about heart, culture, acceptance and embracing? What if our churches were overflowing with the hope of Jesus Christ . . . a hope not simply for those who "fit in" or look the part, but rather a hope to all, including the marginalized, downtrodden and outcast?

Becoming *Irresistible* is more than programs and activities—it is about a transformational work in our hearts . . . first as individuals and then as the body of Christ. *Irresistible* allows us to see each individual as he or she truly is: created in the image of God (Genesis 1:26-27), designed purposely as a masterpiece (Psalm 139:13-14), instilled with purpose, plans and dreams (Jeremiah 29:11), and a truly indispensable member of the kingdom of God (1 Corinthians 12:23). An *Irresistible Church* is an "authentic community built on the hope of Christ that compels people affected by disability to fully belong." It is powerful for a person to know that he or she is fully welcomed and belongs. *Irresistible* captures the heart of the church as it should be—how else do we explain the rapid growth and intense attraction to the church in the book of Acts? The heart of God was embodied through the people of God by the Spirit of God . . . and that is simply *Irresistible*!

The Irresistible Church Series is designed to help not only shape and transform the heart of the church, but also to provide the practical steps and activities to put *flesh* around the *heart* of the church—to help your church become a place for people to fully belong. Thank you for responding to the call to become *Irresistible*. It will not happen overnight, but it will happen. As with all good things, it requires patience and perseverance, determination and dedication, and ultimately an underlying trust in the faithfulness of God. May God bless you on this journey. Be assured that you are not alone—there are many on the path of *Irresistible*.

For more information or to join the community,
please visit www.irresistiblechurch.org.

**Joni and Friends**
INTERNATIONAL DISABILITY CENTER

Joni and Friends was established in 1979 by Joni Eareckson Tada, who at 17 was injured in a diving accident, leaving her a quadriplegic. Since its inception, Joni and Friends has been dedicated to extending the love and message of Christ to people who are affected by disability whether it is the disabled person, a family member, or friend. Our objective is to meet the physical, emotional, and spiritual needs of this group of people in practical ways.

Joni and Friends is committed to recruiting, training, and motivating new generations of people with disabilities to become leaders in their churches and communities. Today, the Joni and Friends International Disability Center serves as the administrative hub for an array of programs which provide outreach to thousands of families affected by disability around the globe. These include two radio programs, an award-winning television series, the Wheels for the World international wheelchair distribution ministry, Family Retreats which provide respite for those with disabilities and their families, Field Services to provide church training along with educational and inspirational resources at a local level, and the Christian Institute on Disability to establish a firm biblical worldview on disability-related issues.

From local neighborhoods to the far reaches of the world, Joni and Friends is striving to demonstrate to people affected by disability, in tangible ways, that God has not abandoned them—he is with them—providing love, hope, and eternal salvation.

# Customizable Resources from the Book

## Available for Download at
http://www.irresistiblechurch.org/library/

# Other Recommended Resources

### *Beyond Suffering Bible*

The *Beyond Suffering Bible* by Joni and Friends is the first study Bible made specifically for those who suffer and the people who love them. Uplifting insights from Joni Eareckson Tada and numerous experts and scholars who have experienced suffering in their own lives and will help you move beyond the "why" of suffering to grasp the eternal value God is building into our lives. Special features include: inspiring devotionals, biblical and contemporary profiles, Bible reading plans, connection points and disability ministry resources.

http://www.joniandfriends.org/store/category/bibles/

### *Beyond Suffering®*
### *Student Edition*

*Beyond Suffering for the Next Generation: A Christian View on Disability Ministry* will equip young people to consider the issues that affect people with disabilities and their families, and inspire them to action. Students who embrace this study will gain confidence to join a growing, worldwide movement that God is orchestrating to fulfill Luke 14:21-23: "Go out quickly into the streets and alleys of the town and bring in the poor, the crippled, the blind, and the lame . . . so that my house will be full."

ISBN: 978-0-9838484-6-2
304 pages · 8.5" x 11"
Includes CD-ROM

http://www.joniandfriends.org/BYSNextGen/

### *Joni:*
### *An Unforgettable Story*

In this unforgettable autobiography, Joni reveals each step of her struggle to accept her disability and discover the meaning of her life. The hard-earned truths she discovers and the special ways God reveals his love are testimonies to faith's triumph over hardship and suffering. This new edition includes an afterword, in which Joni talks about the events that have occurred in her life since the book's original publication in 1976, including her marriage and the expansion of her worldwide ministry to families affected by disability.

ISBN: 978-0310240013
205 pages · Paperback

http://www.joniandfriends.org/blog/joni-book-40-year-anniversary/

# Available Now in the Irresistible Church Series

## Start with Hello
*Introducing Your Church to Special Needs Ministry*

Families with special needs often share that they desire two things in their church: accessibility and acceptance. Accessibility to existing structures, programs and people is an imperative. Acceptance with a sense of belonging by the others who also participate in the structures, programs and fellowship of the church is equally necessary. In this simple book you'll learn the five steps to becoming an accessible and accepting church.

To receive first notice of upcoming resources, including respite, inclusive worship and support groups, please contact us at churchrelations@joniandfriends.org.

# Available Now in the Irresistible Church Series

*We've Got This!*
*Providing Respite for Families Affected by Disability*

Families or caregivers who have children with disabilities are often isolated, exhausted, and grieving. Respite events can be a safe bridge for families to cross over the threshold of the church by satisfying an urgent need. A place for children to be themselves, for caregivers to have a break and for the church to serve well is invaluable. This book is a practical guide that provides the necessary tools to plan and execute a successful respite event.

To receive first notice of upcoming resources, including respite, inclusive worship and support groups, please contact us at churchrelations@joniandfriends.org.

# Available Now in the Irresistible Church Series

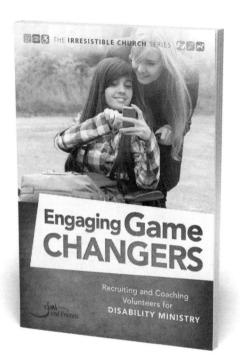

## *Engaging Game Changers*
### *Recruiting and Coaching Volunteers for Disability Ministry*

The breadth of impact any ministry has for the individuals they serve is dependent on the volunteers who are recruited to be the hands and feet of Jesus. This resource will train you as a ministry leader to identify and recruit, thoroughly train, then release volunteers who will serve families affected by special needs effectively and with the love of Christ.

To receive first notice of upcoming resources, including respite, inclusive worship and support groups, please contact us at churchrelations@joniandfriends.org.

# Available Now in the Irresistible Church Series

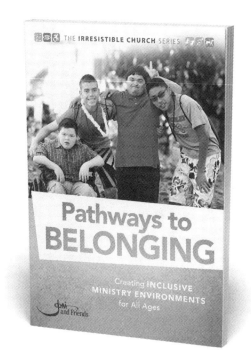

## *Pathways to Belonging*
*Creating Inclusive Ministry Environments for All Ages*

Church leaders with a heart to serve families affected by disability frequently ask, "How do I know the best way to include each special friend when their needs vary?" This book is a response to that question, offering step-by-step tools for evaluating the needs of friends with disabilities and creating a culture that welcomes these individuals and their families. Within these pages, we discuss creating accessible environments that provide access to the gospel while being sensitive to learning styles and physical needs.

To receive first notice of upcoming resources, including respite, inclusive worship and support groups, please contact us at churchrelations@joniandfriends.org.

# Available Now in the Irresistible Church Series

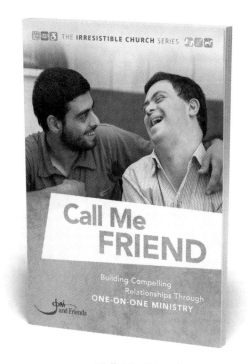

## *Call Me Friend*
*Building Compelling Relationships Through One-on-One Ministry*

For the ministry leader who desires to include people of all ages with special needs in the life of the church, this practical guide to buddy ministry provides clear, concise direction on how to organize and implement this effective ministry model. Leaders will discover how buddies provide discipleship, friendship, safety, participation, communication and positive behavior management. The simple steps you'll find in this book will build relationships and assist your church in becoming an authentic community where all people may fully belong.

To receive first notice of upcoming resources, including respite, inclusive worship and support groups, please contact us at churchrelations@joniandfriends.org.

# Available Now in the Irresistible Church Series

## Shout for JOY!
### *Engaging the Whole Church in Accessible Worship*

Do you long to be part of a church community where people of all abilities gather to worship, a church where the sounds of worship include a wheelchair rolling down the aisle, the tap of a cane, and the sound of people with differing intellectual disabilities lifting their voices together in praise and prayer? If so, we pray that *Shout for Joy!* will help your church have a heart for worship that is accessible to all and give you some practical "how-to" ideas as well.

To receive first notice of upcoming resources, including respite, inclusive worship and support groups, please contact us at churchrelations@joniandfriends.org.